BACKPACK EXPLORER

ROCK HUNT

Storey Publishing

Are You Ready to Be a
ROCK HOUND?

A **rock hound** is a person who likes to look for and collect rocks and minerals. You can search for rocks and minerals almost anywhere. Once you start looking, you're sure to find many different kinds. Load up your backpack, head outside, and start hunting!

THINGS TO BRING IN YOUR BACKPACK

This book and magnifying glass

Sunscreen or hat

Small paintbrush

Small shovel or trowel

Pencil

Snacks and water

HOW TO HAVE FUN WITH THIS BOOK

Learn about different types of ROCKS and MINERALS

Make a PET ROCK

Go on a SCAVENGER HUNT

Use the MAGNIFYING GLASS for a closer look

SKIP STONES across the water

Look for WISHING STONES

Create your own ROCK COLLECTION

ROCK PATCH STICKERS

There are 12 patch stickers in the back of this book that match **I SEE IT!** circles on some of the pages. When you see a type of rock or mineral that matches something on an **I SEE IT!** page, put the sticker on the matching circle. See how many you can find!

Place the sticker on the circle!

Sedimentary Rock

I SEE IT!

WIND, WATER, AND ICE CAN CRUMBLE, OR ERODE, OLD ROCKS OVER TIME. The little pieces of sand and gravel left behind are called sediment. Rainwater and snowmelt wash sediment down into lakes and the ocean. As all those rock bits pile up, the bottom layers get squished together to make a new sedimentary rock.

SHALE layers are easy to pull apart.

Look for different types of **SEDIMENTARY** rock!

Shale is the most common sedimentary rock.

Can you find rocks with distinct layers?

Sandstone

Coal is made from plants that died millions of years ago.

Coal

Limestone is made of old seashells turned into hardened mud.

Limestone

Conglomerate rocks look like clay and pebbles squished together.

Zoom In

How many different shapes and colors do you see?

39

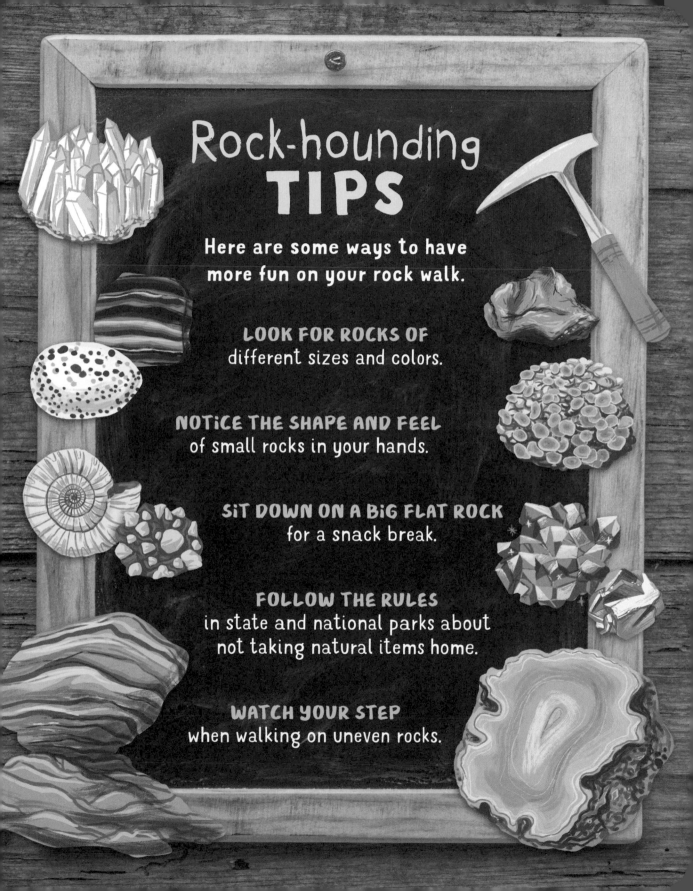

Rock-hounding TIPS

Here are some ways to have more fun on your rock walk.

LOOK FOR ROCKS OF different sizes and colors.

NOTICE THE SHAPE AND FEEL of small rocks in your hands.

SIT DOWN ON A BIG FLAT ROCK for a snack break.

FOLLOW THE RULES in state and national parks about not taking natural items home.

WATCH YOUR STEP when walking on uneven rocks.

Pebbles & Stones

A PEBBLE IS A SMALL STONE, AND STONE IS ANOTHER WORD FOR ROCK. Pebbles are often about the size of a coin. They are smooth with rounded edges and feel nice to hold in your hand. In fact, some people like to carry one in their pocket to use as a worry stone. They think rubbing the stone is relaxing. Find a pebble and give it a try!

Pebbles can be many different colors and shapes.

What kinds of **TINY ROCKS** can you find?

Pick up a handful of pebbles. Do they feel cool or warm?

Can you find a reddish pebble?

Pebbles make great toes!

Can you find a stone as small as a dime?

Can you find some heart-shaped stones?

Hold a bunch of pebbles in your cupped hands and shake them like a rattle!

Zoom In

Water makes stones look more colorful. Grab a bright wet one and watch the color fade as it dries.

Create a
COLLECTION

True rock hounds love to show off their favorite finds. Your rock and mineral collection may include your weirdest, coolest, or most colorful stones—the ones you really want to share. It might also hold special rocks you found on a beach vacation or camping trip, or a visit to a rock shop.

1 You may need to clean up some rocks before you display them. Dip dirty rocks in water or use an old toothbrush to scrub off any dirt or mud. Dust off dry stones with a little paintbrush.

2 Sort your rocks by size, shape, color, or any way that makes sense to you.

3 Put your rocks into egg carton(s).

4 Decorate your collection box with the sticker from the back of this book or make your own label.

Make an outdoor collection and leave it for someone to find!

Boulders

GIANT ROCKS, ONES THAT ARE BIGGER THAN PEOPLE, ARE CALLED BOULDERS. Boulders are not attached to other rocks. Some were carried many miles by glaciers or rivers a long time ago. Others rolled down off mountains. You can find boulders in some surprising places!

Look out below!
Bubble Rock, Acadia National Park, ME

ERRATIC [EH-RA-tic] boulders are different from the rocks around them. Most were moved by glacier ice. Their name comes from a Latin word that means "to wander."

Are there any **BOULDERS** near your home?

Have you ever climbed on a boulder?

Tripod Rock at Pyramid Mountain, NJ

A tumble of boulders

The sport of climbing boulders is called **bouldering**.

This boulder has a tree growing around it!

Sequoia National Park, CA

Yellowstone National Park, WY

Can you find a boulder that looks like a house or a big animal?

Zoom In

Lichen loves to grow on boulders. What does it feel like to touch a crusty lichen mat?

LANDFORMS

Mountains, valleys, and islands are types of natural landforms. Like rocks, these features slowly change shape over time. Rivers and canyons are made when rocks are taken away from an area by water. Erupting volcanoes might create new landforms when their lava cools.

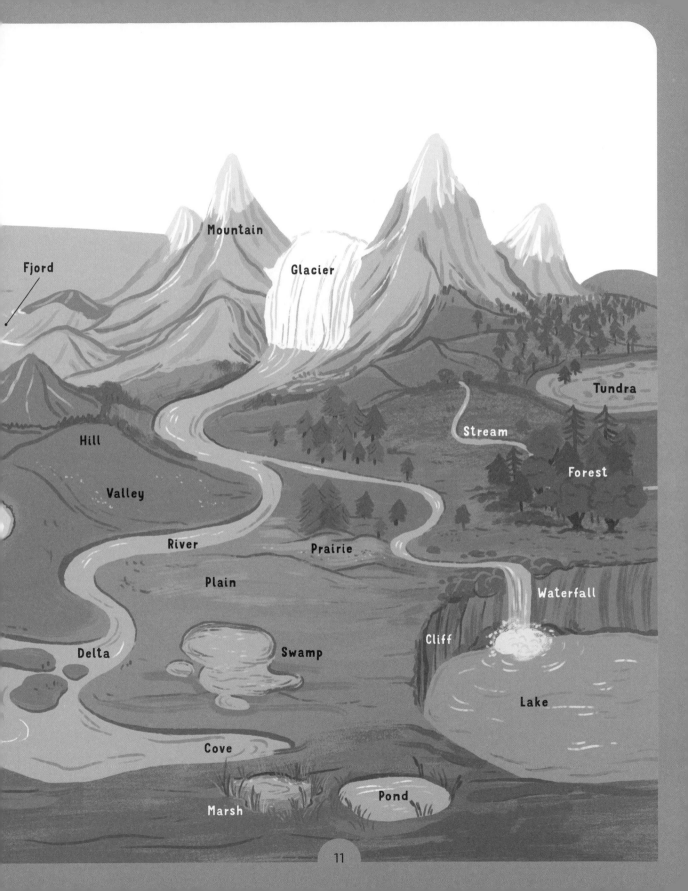

River Rocks & Beach Stones

IF YOU'RE EXPLORING ALONG A LAKESHORE OR RIVERBANK, LOOK FOR SMOOTH, FLAT ROCKS. Flowing water causes rocks to tumble around and bump into each other. All that banging together wears down the rough edges over time. These flat and rounded stones are great for stacking into towers and skipping across the water!

The world record for stone skips is 88!

How many smooth, **ROUNDED STONES** can you find?

Have you ever stacked rocks? See page 36.

Find stones with a white stripe and connect them.

Can you find a round rock?

Look for rocks the color of sand.

Zoom In

Rock tumbler machines work like rivers. They roll rough stones around in water and sand until they are smooth and shiny.

Tumbled agate

ROCK PIRATES and BARK BOATS

Set some pirates off to sea in this fun game that you play by a pond or slow-moving stream. Always be careful around water and make sure an adult is near to help.

1 Find a wide, flat piece of bark for your boat. Collect a few small rocks or pebbles for your pirates.

2 Balance the rock pirates in the middle of your bark boat.

3 Carefully go to the water's edge and gently place your boat into the water.

4 Ahoy, matey! Did your pirates stay on board and sail into the sunset? If they sank, try again!

Try different sizes and numbers of rocks for your pirate crew.

How long can your boat stay afloat?

Sand

SAND IS MADE UP OF TINY PIECES OF ROCK AND MINERALS that have been broken down by water, ice, and wind. A grain of sand may be jagged or rounded, depending on what type of rock it came from. That's why some sand feels soft and smooth, while other sand is rough to the touch.

Sand can be almost any color.

Tan sand is made of quartz crystals tinted by iron.

How many different KINDS OF SAND have you seen?

White sand may be made mostly of tiny quartz crystals.

Reddish-orange sand likely has a lot of iron in it.

Rare green-colored sand contains green minerals like olivine.

Black sand probably came from volcanoes and is made of basalt.

Zoom In

Grab a handful of sand. How many different colors can you find?

Minerals

MINERALS ARE THE BUILDING BLOCKS THAT MAKE ROCKS. Minerals grow as crystals, but each one has a special set of qualities, like its shape, color, and how hard it is. Humans use minerals to make cars, computers, window glass, jewelry, pennies, and more. There are even minerals in your toothpaste!

You have minerals dissolved in your body, like iron in your blood and calcium in your bones!

You can find **MINERALS** almost anywhere!

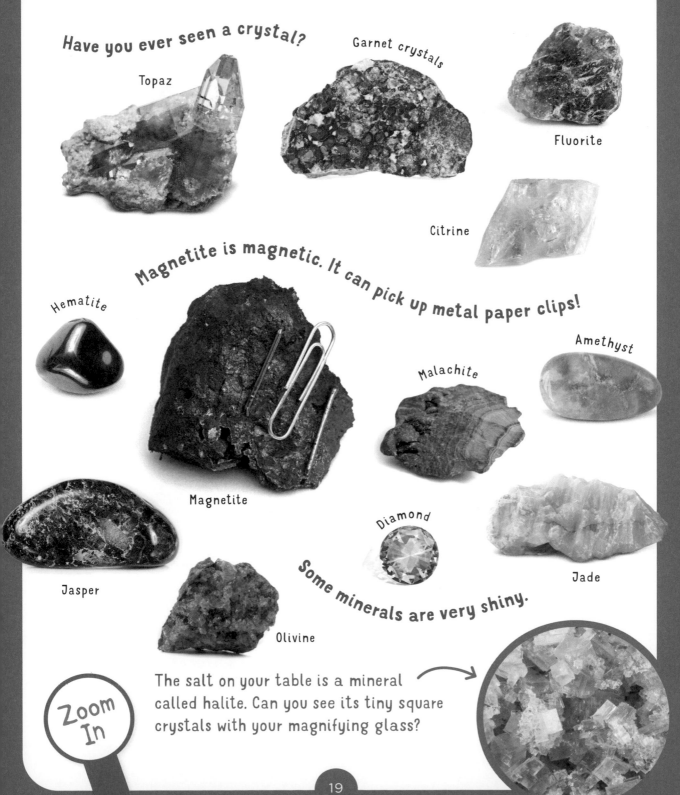

Have you ever seen a crystal?

Topaz

Garnet crystals

Fluorite

Citrine

Magnetite is magnetic. It can pick up metal paper clips!

Hematite

Amethyst

Malachite

Magnetite

Diamond

Jade

Jasper

Some minerals are very shiny.

Olivine

Zoom In

The salt on your table is a mineral called halite. Can you see its tiny square crystals with your magnifying glass?

iDENTiFYiNG MiNERALS

Geologists use different tests to help identify minerals. A mineral's color, smell, and density in water offer clues, but here are some more common tests.

BREAK iT

A **cleavage** test looks at how a mineral breaks apart. Does it break into flat sheets or little crystals?

SHiNE A LiGHT ON iT

If a mineral reflects light and looks shiny like metal, it has a metallic **luster**. If the light passes through, it has a glassy luster. Some minerals have a dull or waxy luster.

STREAK iT

Rubbing the mineral across a clay tile leaves a streak of colored powder. The color of the streak may be different from the chunk of mineral.

SCRATCH iT

Geologists use the **Mohs hardness scale** to test how easy it is to scratch a mineral. You can scratch soft minerals with your fingernail, so they score a 1 or 2 on the scale. A diamond gets a 10 because almost nothing can leave a mark on it.

Can you make scratch marks on any of the rocks you found?

SOFTEST

 1. TALC

 2. GYPSUM

 3. CALCITE

 4. FLUORITE

 5. APATITE

 6. FELDSPAR

 7. QUARTZ

 8. TOPAZ/BERYL

 9. CORUNDUM

 10. DIAMOND

HARDEST

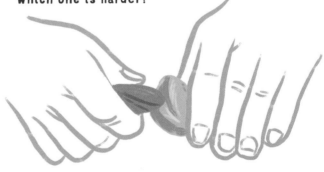

Use your fingernail. If it scratches, it's a soft mineral.

Scratch one mineral on another. Which one is harder?

If your rock doesn't scratch after the first tests, try using a penny. That rock will be hardest.

Quartz

QUARTZ [KWARTS] IS A VERY COMMON MINERAL. It can be transparent (see-through) or opaque (not see-through). Quartz comes in many colors, but the kind you're most likely to find on a walk is plain white milky quartz.

Quartz is hard enough to scratch glass!

How many kinds of **WHITE ROCKS** can you find?

Limestone

White chalk is made from the mineral calcite.

Calcite

Milky quartz

Chalk

Feldspar is a white mineral often used to make glass.

Feldspar

White stones can be shiny or dull.

Marble

Gypsum

Agate

Zoom In

Talcum powder is made of ground-up talc, the softest mineral in the world.

IN DAILY LIFE

Rocks and minerals are used to make many products you might find around home or at school. If you find one of these, check the box!

Salt ☐

Pencil lead ☐

Chalk & chalkboard ☐

Glass ☐

Gold or Silver ☐

Aluminum foil ☐

Granite countertop ☐

Bricks ☐

Iron nail ☐

GEMSTONES!

A gemstone, or gem, is an especially beautiful mineral. Gems are often cut into certain shapes and polished until they sparkle and shine. Rare gems can be very valuable, and they are sometimes used to make fancy jewelry.

You probably won't find many gemstones on your walks, but you can find some cool ones at rock shops and museum gift shops!

Tiger's eye

Carnelian

Agate

Jasper

Aventurine

Ruby

Malachite

Diamond

Emerald

Moonstone

Apatite

Amethyst

Turquoise

Lapis lazuli

Sapphire

Black & Gray Rocks

MANY ROCKS ARE BLACK OR GRAY. One of the most common is basalt, which is found in many different places on the surface of the earth. It also covers a lot of the ocean floor. Basalt forms when lava from a volcano cools and hardens. Although some chunks look holey with air pockets, it's actually a really tough and heavy rock.

Black stones absorb heat from the sun. Can you find one that feels warm to the touch?

Look for different kinds of **GRAY AND BLACK** rocks!

Scoria

Basalt

Look for a smooth gray stone.

Shale breaks easily if you drop it.

Flint

Shale

Find six gray rocks and line them up like a herd of tiny elephants!

Pumice

Onyx

Zoom In

Coal is made of the fossil remains of ancient plants. It looks shiny when you break it apart.

MY PET ROCK

When you're out hunting for rocks, look for special ones that you can make into a new friend!

1 Start with a smooth stone or flat rock to make your pet's body or face.

2 Gather leaves, pinecones, small twigs, and pebbles. Use them to create legs, wings, or whiskers for your pet. Seeds, nuts, and berries make good eyes.

3 Tell a little story about your pet. What is its name? What does it eat?

Keep your pet warm with a leaf blanket or stick tent.

Give a boulder a face!

Striped & Speckled Stones

STRIPED STONES ARE FUN TO FIND. It almost looks like someone painted the lines on them. Some people even believe a stone with an unbroken stripe of quartz running all the way around it grants wishes. Have you ever found a wishing rock? Did your wish come true?

Big boulders and canyon walls can be made of striped stone.

Art in Nature
Rattlesnake Canyon, AZ

Find stones with STRIPES, SPECKLES, and SPOTS!

The lines and dots are different types of minerals.

Dalmatian stone

Petrified wood is often striped.

Look for stones with a circle, an X, or other lines.

Can you find a rock with two stripes?

Cut agate shows the stripes inside.

Quartz stripes

Moss agate

Zoom In

Look closely at a speckled stone. Are there different colored flecks or are they all the same color?

ROCK ART

DRAW SHAPES OR LETTERS

on the sidewalk with chalk, or use a stick to draw in the dirt or sand. Cover your drawing with small pebbles.

PAINT A ROCK WITH WATER

and then watch your art slowly disappear as it dries.

MAKE A HEART and fill it in

with small pebbles. Take a picture and send it to someone you love!

ARRANGE ROCK FLOWERS

on a flat surface.

COLOR & PATTERNS

Rocks and minerals can be dull or shiny, and they come in all sorts of colors and patterns. If you spot any of these types on a rock hunt, check the box.

SPOTTED ☐

DULL ☐

MULTICOLORED ☐

BLACK ☐

WHITE ☐

ORANGE ☐

GREEN ☐

SPARKLY ☐

STRIPED ☐

Sparkly Rocks

SOME ROCKS SEEM TO SPARKLE AS IF THEY WERE DIPPED IN GLITTER. Look carefully and you will see that the twinkling might come from spots of minerals like mica [MY-kuh] or quartz. Those shiny flecks reflect sunlight like tiny mirrors and make the rock glimmer.

If the flecks look like shiny metal, they might be pyrite, or "fool's gold."

Can you find some **SPARKLY** rocks?

Sparkly flecks are made of different minerals.

Hematite

Use a flashlight to look closer at all those sparkles!

Geodes look like dull rocks on the outside but sparkle inside.

Rutilated quartz

Rose quartz

Peacock ore is a colorful mineral you aren't likely to find in your yard unless you live near a copper mine.

Some schist looks like it's covered in glitter.

Peacock ore

Zoom In

Mica is made of layers and layers of thin flat crystals you can peel apart.

STACKING STONES

You can have fun sorting or stacking stones in just about any way you can think of! Try these ideas, then come up with some of your own.

STONE WALLS

Put the biggest, flattest rocks on the bottom, and build up layer by layer.

Try making an archway!

ROCK TOWERS

A stack of rocks is called a **CAIRN**. How many stones can you stack? How many flat stones can you balance on your hand?

Some big parks ask people not to make cairns, so be sure to know the rules. Sometimes picking up rocks disturbs insects and animals who live under them.

If you make a stack, put them back!

Sedimentary Rock

I SEE IT!

WIND, WATER, AND ICE CAN CRUMBLE, OR ERODE, OLD ROCKS OVER TIME. The little pieces of sand and gravel left behind are called sediment. Rainwater and snowmelt wash sediment down into lakes and the ocean. As all those rock bits pile up, the bottom layers get squished together to make a new sedimentary rock.

SHALE layers are easy to pull apart.

Look for different types of **SEDIMENTARY** rock!

Shale is the most common sedimentary rock.

Can you find rocks with distinct layers?

Sandstone

Coal is made from plants that died millions of years ago.

Coal

Limestone is made of old seashells turned into hardened mud.

Limestone

Conglomerate rocks look like clay and pebbles squished together.

Zoom In

How many different shapes and colors do you see?

ROCK CYCLE

Rocks aren't alive, but they do change over time. All the rocks on Earth eventually turn into a different kind of rock. This is called the rock cycle, and it can take millions or billions of years to complete.

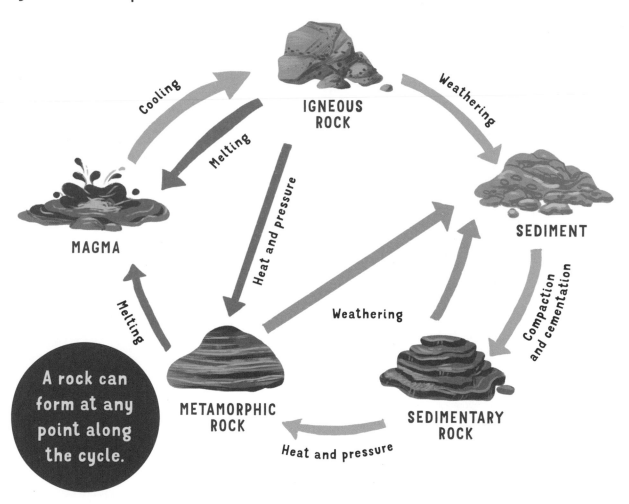

Cooling

IGNEOUS ROCK

Weathering

Melting

Heat and pressure

MAGMA

SEDIMENT

Melting

Weathering

Compaction and cementation

A rock can form at any point along the cycle.

METAMORPHIC ROCK

SEDIMENTARY ROCK

Heat and pressure

Earth's surface layer, or **crust**, is made up of giant puzzle pieces called plates. As those plates rub against each other, they squeeze rocks between them, pushing up mountains or burying rock deep below the surface.

MELTING: Rocks that get buried deep in the earth melt into hot liquid **magma**. When that magma cools underground or after it shoots out of a volcano as **lava**, it forms **igneous rock**.

WEATHERING: Aboveground, wind and water slowly break down all kinds of rocks into little pieces called **sediment**. Those bits wash into lakes or oceans. Eventually they are pressed into **sedimentary rock**.

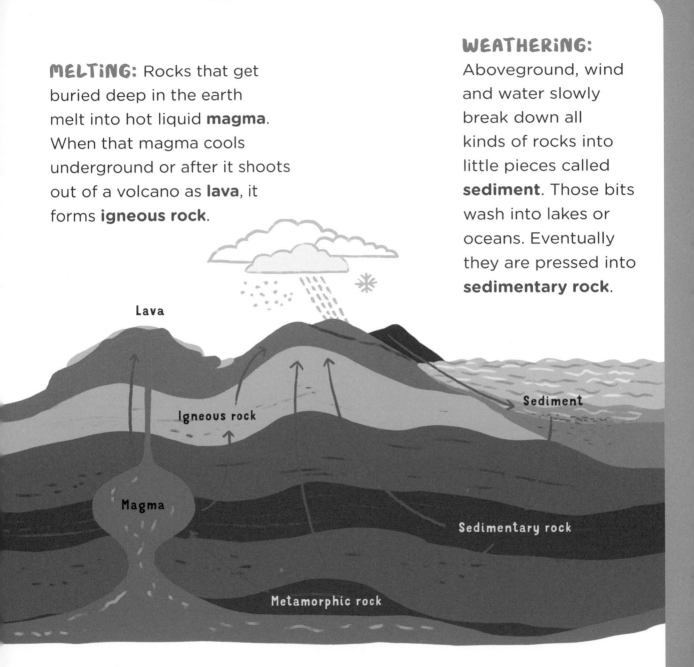

Lava

Igneous rock

Sediment

Magma

Sedimentary rock

Metamorphic rock

SQUEEZING: Metamorphic rock has been heated and squeezed under a huge amount of pressure below the surface.

Metamorphic Rock

THE WORD **METAMORPHOSIS** MEANS "A CHANGE OF SHAPE." You probably know it from the way a caterpillar transforms into a butterfly. So how does a metamorphic rock change? As the earth's surface plates slowly shift, they crush and squeeze buried rocks between them. All that heat and pressure changes the rock into a different form.

Have you ever seen a white statue at a museum? It was probably made of metamorphic marble.

METAMORPHIC ROCKS can look very different.

Marble

Soapstone is soft and easy to carve.

Soapstone

Lapis lazuli powder was once used to make blue paint!

Lapis lazuli

Schist

Teachers used to use slate for chalkboards.

Quartzite

Slate

Some metamorphic rocks look twisted or bent.

Zoom In

Can you see wavy-looking bands in your rock?

FOSSILS ARE STONES!

Fossils are the very old remains of dead plants and animals preserved in rock. Petrified wood is a fossil. See the photo on page 31.

TRACE FOSSILS

come from super-old animal signs, like footprints, eggs, or even poop! These fossils give scientists clues about how animals lived millions of years ago.

Fossilized footprints

An egg fossil

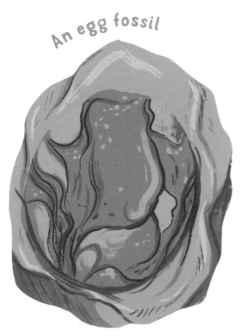

Poop fossils are called **coprolites**!

BODY FOSSILS formed from ancient bones, shells, and teeth or hard bits of wood. Dinosaur skeletons are body fossils.

The word **fossil** means "dug up."

Have you ever seen a fossil?

This **Petoskey stone** is a body fossil of coral.

Igneous Rock

VERY FAR BENEATH THE EARTH IS A LAYER OF SUPER-HOT MELTED ROCK CALLED MAGMA. As it cools down it hardens into igneous rock. These rocks tend to be very hard and smooth and are often found near volcanoes. When the liquid magma reaches the surface, we call it lava.

Volcanic rocks form when liquid magma cools and hardens on the earth's surface.

Can you find different types of **IGNEOUS** rock?

Obsidian is smooth and shiny, but its sharp edges can cut.

Obsidian

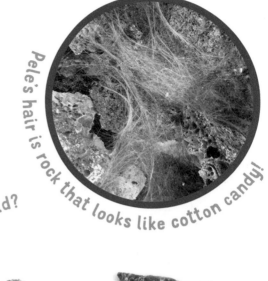

Pele's hair is rock that looks like cotton candy!

Have you ever seen an obsidian arrowhead?

Felsite

Peridotite

Dunite

Diorite rocks have a salt-and-pepper look.

Volcanic basalt

Diorite

Zoom In

Pumice is full of tiny holes. All those little pockets of air make this rock light enough to float!

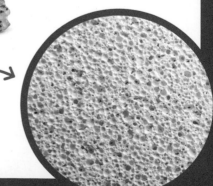

HOW DOES IT FEEL?

Reach out and touch every rock you see. How do they feel against your hand? Check off each texture you find.

ROUGH ☐

SMOOTH ☐

ROUNDED ☐

BUMPY ☐

CRACKED ☐

HOLEY ☐

POINTY ☐

WARM ☐

COOL ☐

MY ROCK HOUND JOURNAL

Pick your favorite rock from your rock-hunting adventures and describe why you like it.

THIS IS MY ROCK! Draw a picture of your rock or put a photo of it here.

Where I found my rock

Why I like my rock

Dalmatian stone

Geode

Quartz

Fossil

Onyx

Amethyst

ROCK PATCH STICKERS

Look for these different kinds of rocks and minerals. When you spot one, place your sticker on the matching circle where it says, "I SEE IT!"

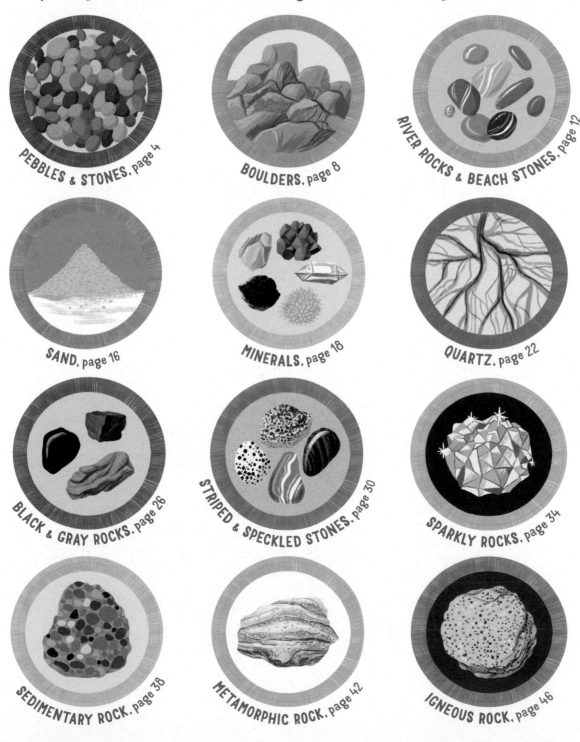

PEBBLES & STONES, page 4

BOULDERS, page 8

RIVER ROCKS & BEACH STONES, page 12

SAND, page 16

MINERALS, page 18

QUARTZ, page 22

BLACK & GRAY ROCKS, page 26

STRIPED & SPECKLED STONES, page 30

SPARKLY ROCKS, page 34

SEDIMENTARY ROCK, page 38

METAMORPHIC ROCK, page 42

IGNEOUS ROCK, page 46

The mission of Storey Publishing is to serve our customers by
publishing practical information that encourages
personal independence in harmony with the environment.

Text by Kathleen Yale
Edited by Deanna F. Cook and Lisa H. Hiley
Art direction and book design by Erin Dawson
Text production by Jennifer Jepson Smith

Cover and interior illustrations by © Oana Befort
Interior photography by Mars Vilaubi © Storey Publishing, LLC
Additional stock photography by © Africa Studio/stock.adobe.com, 25 (lapis), 27 (onyx); © agefotostock/Alamy Stock Photo, 19 (magnetite); © ala/stock.adobe.com, 35 (rutilated quartz); © aleks-p/stock.adobe.com, 23 (limestone), 2 & 39 (limestone); © Alex Ekins Adventure Photography/Alamy Stock Photo, 9 t.c.; © AlexStar/iStock.com, 27 (six gray rocks); © Alisa/stock.adobe.com, 23 (chalk); © AlxeyPnferov/iStock.com, 27 (shale); © AmySachar/Shutterstock.com, 17 (black inset); © Andreas Wass/stock.adobe.com, 47 (volcanic basalt); © AndreasKermann/iStock.com, 19 (malachite); © Anna Usova/iStock.com, 19 (citrine); © AskinTulayOver/iStock.com, 48 m.c.; © benedek/iStock.com, 25 (malachite); © bonniemarie/stock.adobe.com, 9 m.r.; © Bozena Fulawka/stock.adobe.com, 13 b.r.; © Çağla Köhserli/iStock.com, 35 (hematite); © Catherine Delahaye/Getty Images, 18; © Chris LaBasco/iStock.com, 30; © Cobalt/stock.adobe.com, 48 b.c.; © DanaDaglePhotography/stock.adobe.com, 13 t.l.; © Daniel/stock.adobe.com, 25 (peacock ore); © Daryl Baird/Unsplash, 37 b.l.; © David Makharashvili/Dreamstime.com, 9 t.r.; © David R./Alamy Stock Photo, pull out (background); © Dominic Fial/iStock.com, 35 (schist); © donatas1205/stock.adobe.com, 13 b.c.r.; © duke2015/stock.adobe.com, 9 t.l.; © edb3_16/stock.adobe.com, 5 b.r.; © Ekaterina/stock.adobe.com, 23 (feldspar), 43 (soapstone); © ekramar/stock.adobe.com, 13 2nd from t.l. & b.c.l.; © Elnur/stock.adobe.com, 13 t.r.; © epitavi/stock.adobe.com, 19 (amethyst), 23 (agate), 25, (aventurine); © ericdalecreative/123RF.com, 17 (green); © evegenesis/stock.adobe.com, 2 & 39 (coal); © Evgenii S/stock.adobe.com, 22; © eyewave/stock.adobe.com 3 (background); © Galka3250/stock.adobe.com, 25 (apatite); © gamjai/stock.adobe.com, 19 (jade); © GeorgeBurba/iStock.com, 48 t.l.; © Gina Easley/Stockimo/Alamy Stock Photo, 35 (geode); © gmstockstudio/stock.adobe.com, 13 t.c.; © Hafiez Razali/Alamy Stock Photo, 17 b.r.; © horstgerlach/iStock.com, 31 (2nd fr.t.l., 2nd fr.t.m.l. & 2nd fr.t.m.r.); © Igor Stevanovic/Alamy Stock Photo, 17 (white inset); © ikostudio/stock.adobe.com, 26; © iluzia/stock.adobe.com, 25 (jasper); © J.C.Salvadores/stock.adobe.com, 19 (fluorite); © Jake Nackos/Unsplash, 4; © jeffwqc/stock.adobe.com, 47 (arrowhead); © Joel Papalini/iStock.com, 27 (olivine); © joey333/stock.adobe.com, 2 & 39 (sandstone); © jonnysek/stock.adobe.com, 31 b.l.; © Julian Popov/EyeEm/Getty Images, 23 b.r.; © julien ratel/Getty Images, 46; © kavring/stock.adobe.com, 43 (schist); © klamatatratip/stock.adobe.com, 25 (sapphire); © Konstanze Gruber/stock.adobe.com, 43 b.r.; © Krzysztof Bubel/stock.adobe.com, 31 (quartz stripes); © KYNA STUDIO/stock.adobe.com, 48 m.l.; © Kyryl Gorlov/Alamy Stock Photo, 2 & 38; © Layne Kennedy/Getty Images, 34; © Leonid Tit/stock.adobe.com, 17 (black); © lissart/iStock.com, 35 (mica); © Lokibaho/iStock.com, 8; © Lost_in_the_Midwest/stock.adobe.com, 31 (petrified wood); © LUC KOHNEN/stock.adobe.com, 17 (reddish); © LVV/iStock.com, 25 (turquoise); © marcel/stock.adobe.com, 23 (gypsum); © Marek Kosmal/stock.adobe.com, 19 (hematite); © marekuliasz/iStock.com, 17 (reddish inset); © mariusFM77/iStock.com, 19 b.r.; © mates/stock.adobe.com, 47 (obsidian); © Matveev_Aleksandr/iStock.com, 48 t.r.; © michal812/stock.adobe.com, 27 (basalt); © MIGUEL GARCIA SAAVED/stock.adobe.com, 43 (slate); © Minakryn Ruslan/stock.adobe.com, 25 (carnelian); © Minakryn Ruslan/iStock.com, 19 (jasper); © NASA Image Collection/Alamy Stock Photo, 47 (Pele's hair); © Наталья Плеханова/stock.adobe.com, 5 (heart-shape, l.), 13 m.c.l.) t.c.l.; © Nastya22/iStock.com, 31 (moss agate); © nd700/stock.adobe.com, 31 b.r.; © New Africa/stock.adobe.com, 25 (agate, amethyst), 47

(pumice); © Nicholas Piccillo/stock.adobe.com, 2 & 39 (shale); © Nick/stock.adobe.com, 2 & 39 b.r.; © Oleg Elkov/Alamy Stock Photo, 42; © Oleg1824f/stock.adobe.com, 27 (pumice); © Oliver Mohr/stock.adobe.com, 43 (lapis lazuli); © pabradyphoto/iStock.com, 17 (white); © photo_HYANG/stock.adobe.com, 47 (felsite); © photoworld/stock.adobe.com, 25 (emerald); © Pixel-Shot/stock.adobe.com, 25 (ruby); © Poramet/stock.adobe.com, 13 m.r.; © PPAMPicture/iStock.com, 7 b.; © Probuxtor/stock.adobe.com, 48 b.l.; © Ratchapoom Anupongpan/Dreamstime.com, 16; © Reload Studio/stock.adobe.com, 31 (dalmatian stone); © ROMAN_P/stock.adobe.com, 9 b.r.; © S_E/stock.adobe.com, 19 (garnet); © Sally Wallis/stock.adobe.com, 27 b.r.; © samopauser/stock.adobe.com, 2 & 39 (conglomerate); © Sarayut Hyongsit/Shutterstock.com, 48 m.r.; © sdbower/stock.adobe.com, 13 (tumbled rocks); © Siim Sepp/Alamy Stock Photo, 17 (green inset); © skynesher/iStock.com, 12; © somchaisom/stock.adobe.com, 5 (dime); © supachai/stock.adobe.com, 19 (diamond), 25 (diamond); © Tamara Kulikova/stock.adobe.com, 27 (scoria); © Tao Wu/stock.adobe.com, 35 (rose quartz); © underworld111/iStock.com, 47 (peridotite); © Vera NewSib/stock.adobe.com, 13 b.l.; © vvoe/stock.adobe.com, 19 (topaz), 23, (calcite, marble, milky quartz), 25 (moonstone, tiger's eye), 43 (marble, quartzite), 47 (dunite), 48 t.c.; © VvoeVale/iStock.com, 47 (diorite); © welcomia/123RF.com, 9 m.l.; © William WANG/stock.adobe.com, 13 m.c.; © WONGSAKORN/stock.adobe.com, 48 b.r.; © yauhenka/stock.adobe.com, 27 (flint)

Storey books are available at special discounts when purchased in bulk for premiums and sales promotions as well as for fund-raising or educational use. Special editions or book excerpts can also be created to specification. For details, please call 800-827-8673, or send an email to sales@storey.com.

Storey Publishing
210 MASS MoCA Way
North Adams, MA 01247
storey.com

Printed in China by R.R. Donnelley
10 9 8 7 6 5 4 3 2 1

Library of Congress Cataloging-in-Publication Data on file